Patrick S. Gilmore

Salem Band Leader   1855 – 1858

Patrick S. Gilmore

Salem Band Leader   1855 – 1858

Researched and Compiled by

ROBERT E. STROM

SELF-PUBLISHED IN SALEM, MASSACHUSETTS

ISBN 979-8-9895726-3-2

Printed in the United States

Self-Published in
Salem, Massachusetts

Website: Bobandjenstrom.com
email: Bobstrom10@comcast.net

To my family:
Jennifer, Eric, Emily,
Eleanor, Lena James,
Dana, Felicia,
and Rosie

Content

Introduction ix

Good News From Home
by Patrick S. Gilmore xi

Appendix

INTRODUCTION

One evening, after a Zoom presentation on my first book, *Old Salem in Ballad and Song*, Salem High Band Leader Cynthia Napierkowski mentioned that each year, the music department at Salem High School gave an award that recognizes excellent musicianship and dedication to a Salem High student. That award was named the *Patrick S. Gilmore Band Award*. That conversation led to this project, Patrick S. Gilmore's time in Salem, Massachusetts, as bandleader of the *Salem Brass Band*. While researching, I could not find a comprehensive source for Gilmore's time in Salem since his presence in Salem was brief, but his leadership led the *Salem Brass Band* to national status. Most of my research focuses on local newspapers of the day, the published sheet music Gilmore produced during his time in Salem, and research conducted and collected by Professor of Music Theory at the Boston Conservatory, Jim Dalton and Gilmore ephemera collector and researcher Jarlath MacNamara.

The *Salem Brass Band* was organized in Salem in 1837 with Mr. George W. Felton as leader. Sometime in 1849, the band secured the leadership of Mr. Jerome H. Smith until 1855, when Gilmore came to Salem to lead the band. Gilmore led the band for only 3 years, and when he left Salem, the band continued under the leadership of Mr. Kehrbahn. The *Salem Brass Band* then chose John Parsons as leader. In 1870, Jean M. Missud became a member of the band. In 1878, Jean Missud left the *Salem Bass Band*, organized the *Salem Cadet Band,* and led the band for the next 63 years.* After Missud's death, Salem resident George Rigby continued the marching band tradition in Salem with his band, *Rigby's Band*, until his death some 30 years later. (Rigby donated Missud's Drum, personal diaries, and compositions to the Phillips Library, now in Rowley, Massachusetts) Beginning in 1987 and continuing today, Cynthia Napierkowski has kept the marching band tradition in Salem alive.

Patrick S. Gilmore is remembered today for his efforts galvanizing the country with his two grand concerts, the *World's Peace Jubilee* and the *National Peace Jubilee*. His time in Salem has not gone unnoticed, and he continues to inspire Salem High School Band students as they work toward musical excellence.

~ Bob Strom

[**Essex Institute Historical Collections, Bands and*
Band Music in Salem, Vol. 36, 1900, p. 265 – 284 – RS]

Good News From Home

Good news from home, good news for me,
　　Has come across the deep blue sea.
From friends that I have left in tears,
　　For friends that I have not seen in years.
And since we parted long ago,
　　My life has been a scene of woe,
But now a joyful hour has come,
　　For I have heard good news from home.

Chorus: Good news from home, good news for me,
　　Has come across the deep blue sea.
From friends that I have left in tears,
　　For friends that I have not seen in years.

No fathers near to guide me now,
　　No mother's tear to soothe my brow,
No sister's voice falls on my ear,
　　Nor brother's smile to give me cheer;
But tho' I wander far away,
　　My heart is filled with joy today,
For friends across the ocean foam,
　　Have sent me good news from home. Chorus:

When shall I see the cottage door?
　　Where I spend years of joy before,
'Twas then I knew no grief or care,
　　My heart was always happy there;
Though I may never see it more,
　　Or stand upon my native shore,
Where e'er on earth I'm doomed to roam,
　　My heart will be with those at home. Chorus:

PATRICK S. GILMORE – 1854

Patrick S. Gilmore

Salem Band Leader   1855 – 1858

Patrick S. Gilmore
Time in Salem 1855 – 1858

Essex Institute Historical Collection,
courtesy of the Salem Public Library

Born in Ballygar, County Galway, in 1829, Gilmore emigrated from Ireland to Boston in 1849. Coming to America with a strong background in music, his musical talents and ambitions became apparent, and he soon became the leader of the *Boston Brigade Band*. Gilmore's reputation grew as a bandleader, and his endeavors widened.[1]

While leader of the Boston and Charlestown bands, Gilmore wrote and published several compositions. *The Everlasting Polka,* played by the *Suffolk Brass Band* and penned by Gilmore in 1852 and dedicated to Miss S.E. Daily. During this period, Gilmore also wrote the larger piece, *On The Road To Salem Quick Step,* which includes the *Salem Hornpipe,* a tune still played today, possibly anticipating his move to Salem.

In early 1854, Gilmore wrote *Sad News From Home*[2] and dedicated the song to Miss Maria Hall. Another piece, *Good News from Home,* is a ballad written in 1854 by Gilmore and dedicated to his mother.

In the fall of 1854, Mr. Jerome H. Smith, leader of the *Salem Brass Band*, took sick and soon passed away. On January 15, 1855, the *Salem Register* reported that Gilmore, leader of the *Boston Brigade Band*, "has accepted the leadership of the *Salem Brass Band.*"[3] The newspaper article continued saying that Gilmore was a gentleman and highly qualified for the position.

Sad News From Home, courtesy of Lester S. Levy Collection of Sheet Music, Sheridan Libraries, Johns Hopkins University

3

The Early Days of
The Salem Brass Band

One year after Gilmore left Salem and headed back to Boston, the *Salem Register* published an article called *The Early Days of The Salem Brass Band* [4] outlining the history of the *Salem Brass Band* from its inception in 1837 to 1859.

Transcribed from the *Salem Register:*

The *Salem Brass Band* was organized in 1837, with Mr. George W. Felton as Leader, who, with twelve others, constituted the band at the time. The next season, Mr. F. W. Morse received and accepted a call as Leader and Director, who, although a young man not quite twenty years of age, possessed fine musical talent and taste and united at once, energetically and full of interest, with his associates, to raise the band to quite a degree of excellence. He succeeded in this is evident from the fact that the band received, at home and abroad, a very good share of patronage, being employed by the military, fire, and other associations. The band, too, during his connection with them, performed for Commencement services at Colleges and Universities. In 1848 and '49, the band was obliged to procure a substitute for Mr. Morse as Leader being seized with sickness, which finally proved fatal. He was a good musician, as all must know who ever heard his unsurpassed Bugle and Cornet tones.

Sometime in 1849, the band procured the services of Mr. Jerome H. Smith as leader, who came highly recommended, and all who remember his unrivaled execution and had become acquainted with his genial and gentlemanly manners, together with his great business tact were not surprised that he, too, fully sustained the growing reputation of the band.

It is proper for him, perhaps, to state, as evidence of the popularity of Messers. Morse and Smith, that the citizens of Salem presented to each, at different times, a splendid silver Bugle.

In the fall of 1854, Mr. Smith was suddenly taken sick and, after a short illness, died, lamented, and mourned by all who knew him.

Mr. P.S. Gilmore succeeded Mr. Smith. Heretofore, the principal melody instruments were Bugles, but Mr. Gilmore's joining the band, he being a fine Cornet player and musician, as is well-known bugles were laid aside and Cornets substituted. This was done at some sacrifice, as Messrs. Parsons and Faxon possessed fine silver Bugles. The change was also an improvement doubtless, the Cornet being in every way superior to the Bugle. As the band had increased in experience, ability, and numbers and enjoyed the undivided support and exertion of all the members, it was a comparatively easy task for Mr. Gilmore, with his fine taste and tact, to further develop the talent and extend the patronage of the band, which has certainly attained a reputation second to no other in New England, to say the least. At the close of the present season (1858), Mr. Gilmore decided to move to Boston, and Mr. Kehrbahn was chosen as his successor. [4]

Salem Hornpipe
On The Road To Salem Quick Step

On the Road to Salem,
courtesy of the Boston Public Library

Patrick S. Gilmore wrote the *Salem Hornpipe* [5] in 1853. Jim Dalton, Salem resident and Professor of Core Studies at Boston Conservatory at Berklee, unearthed an early written version of the tune at the Phillips Library in Rowley, Massachusetts. He discovered that the *Salem Hornpipe* was part of a longer piece called *On The Road To Salem Quick Step*. Dalton stated in an article published in the *Salem Gazette*, "The names of the officers were listed in order of rank, right on the music as if Gilmore was dedicating a few beats of the music to each." [6] Dalton continued looking for the connection and noticed, "On the fourth page of the music, it was labeled *Road to Salem*, the same tune as the *Salem Hornpipe*." [6] Elias Howe published the *Salem Hornpipe* in Boston in 1883 and included the tune in *Ryan's Mammoth Collection: 1050 Reels and Jigs* by William Bradbury. Jim and Maggi Smith-Dalton perform 19th and 20th century American music.

Salem Hornpipe, courtesy of Jim and Maggi Dalton's private collection

Gilmore Concerts with
The Salem Brass Band

Soon after Gilmore moved to Salem to lead the *Salem Brass Band*, the *Boston Herald* published an advertisement promoting a complimentary Ball at Union Hall in honor of Gilmore and his leadership role with the *Boston Brigade Band*.[7]

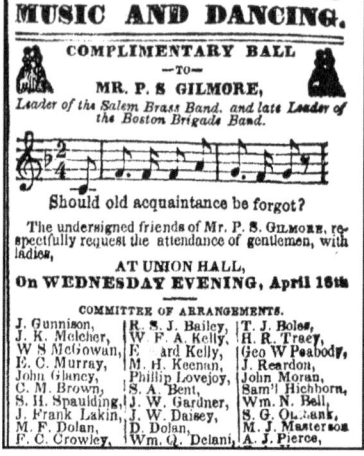

Boston Herald, March 30, 1855

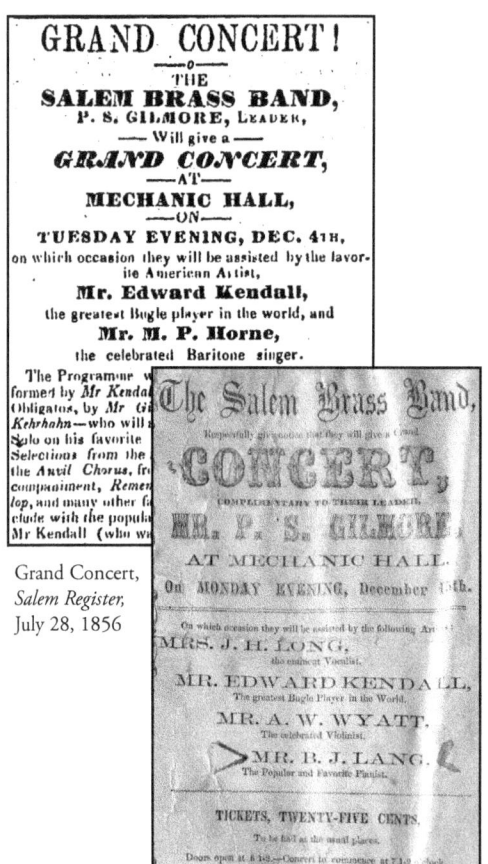

Grand Concert,
Salem Register,
July 28, 1856

Over the next couple of years, Gilmore and the *Salem Brass Band* toured all over New England, building a nationwide reputation as one of the best bands in the country. In 1855, Gilmore put on a Grand Concert at *Mechanics Hall* in Salem featuring Bugle solos by Edward "Ned" Kendall and baritone singer H.P. Horne.[8]

The Salem Brass Band, Concert poster, from the Smith Family Scrapbook [9]

Gilmore continued writing ballads and putting them to music. He published several compositions in 1855 while leading the *Salem Brass Band*, including *Come Buy the Bridal Ring*, *Oh Let Me Dream of Former Years*, and *The Prize Baby Polka*.

Gilmore's productivity continued in 1856, publishing several compositions, including the songs *Music is the Only Charm* and *Bonnie Woman's Smile*. In July of 1856, the *Salem Register* reported that Gilmore's Band put on a public concert on Gallows Hill in Salem with views of downtown and the harbor, adding, "From the eminence, and the elevation is such, and the atmosphere was so clear on Friday, the music could be heard favorably in almost every part of the city." [10]

The following is the programme for to-morrow evening:

PROGRAMME.

PART I.

1—March—On the road to Salem. Gilmore.
2—Pot Pourri—Remembrance of the Military. Weiprecht.
3—Belgian Gallery Polka. Dodworth.
4—Grand Fantaisie for E flat Cornet, variations on Old Folks at Home. Belsheim.
5—Jessamine Waltzes. Labitzky.
6—Divertissement from Robert le Diable. Meyerbeer.

PART II.

7—Grand Selection from Il Trovatore. Verdi.
8—When the Swallows homeward fly. Abt.
9—Wedding March. Mendelssohn.
10—Serenade—Departed Days. Louis.
11—Prize B-by Polka. Gilmore.
12—Grand Finale—National Airs. Jonathan.

Program at Gallows Hill,
Salem Register, July 28, 1856

Gilmore's popularity grew while he led the *Salem Brass Band*. One reason was his ability to know what the people wanted to hear. In the program booklet of his *Grand Concert by Gilmore's Salem Brass Band*, Gilmore performed a sampling of classical pieces, popular songs of the day, and brass band pieces such as marches and quicksteps. [11]

GRAND CONCERT
BY
Gilmore's Salem Brass Band,
Monday Evening February 16, 1857.

PROGRAMME.
PART I.

1—Overture, "I'm Diavolo,"..............................Auber
BRASS BAND.
2—Obligato for B Flat Cornet, from "Domino Noir,".....Donizetti
Mr. L. NEWINGER.
3—Divertisement from "Robert le Diable,".......Meyerbeer
BRASS BAND
4—Two Pieces..........................
No. 1—Song, "I've Waited for thy Coming,"........W. V. Wallace
No. 2—New England Church Polka, dedicated to Capt. G. T. Lyman, P. S. Gilmore
ORCHESTRA.
5—Solo for E Flat Cornet, Fantasia on Old Folks, &c., T. G. Belsheim
Mr. P. S. GILMORE.
6—Grand Duo for Violins,.............................Stahl
Messrs. A. W. WYATT and L. NEWINGER.
7—Marien Waltz,.....................................Gung'l
BRASS BAND.

PART II.

8—Scotch Medley..Knaebel
BRASS BAND.
9—Trumpet Solo, Variations on a Swiss Air...........Kehrhahn
Mr. H. KEHRHAHN.
10—Pot Pourri, Battle of Sebastopol................Weiprecht
BRASS BAND.
11—Quadrille, La Reine di Navarre...................Bohlman
ORCHESTRA.
12—Anvil Chorus, from "Il Trovatore,".................Verdi
BRASS BAND.
13—Battle Galop ....Lieder
BRASS BAND.
14—Grand Finale, "Rogers' Quickstep,"...............Dodworth
Dedicated to the Boston Light Infantry. The Band will wear their new overcoats and big caps during its performance.

Doors open at 7, Concert commences at 7 1-2 o'clock.

Times Job Office—J. H. & F. V. Farwell, & G. Forrest, Printers, 2 and 3 State St., Boston.

Grand Concert – Gilmore's *Salem Brass Band*,
courtesy of Jarlath MacNamara

Gilmore's trip to Washington, DC
with the Salem Brass Band

On March 2, 1857, Gilmore's Band headed to Washington, D.C., and performed at U.S. President James Buchanan's inauguration. *The Salem Register* reported:

Off for Washington, D.C.: A large crowd assembled at the (Salem) Depot on Saturday morning to see Gilmore's Band off and hear their parting notes. There was so much delay, however, from untoward circumstances that they were unable to play more than a couple of pieces, after which they were greeted with a parting salute of six cheers, and the train bore them away. They will probably be absent ten or twelve days on their trip to Washington.[12]

> OFF FOR WASHINGTON. A large crowd of people assembled at the Depot on Saturday morning, to see Gilmore's Band off and hear their parting notes. There was so much delay, however, from untoward circumstances, that they were unable to play more than a couple of pieces, after which they were greeted with a parting salute of six cheers, and the train bore them away. They will probably be absent ten or twelve days on their trip to Washington.

Salem Register, March 2, 1857

The *Salem Register* reported on March 9, 1857, that Gilmore's *Salem Brass Band* appears to have well sustained its reputation abroad. The Washington correspondent of the *Boston Journal* wrote saying:

This morning, Gilmore's Band astonished the natives on Pennsylvania Avenue as the *Charlestown City Guard* marched to the White House. They "stacked arms" and marched into the East Room, where Captain Pierce made a neat address to the President, who replied in his usual happy style. He then shook hands with every member of the Corps and introduced Gen. Shields, who was present. After re-forming out of doors, the Guard fired a salute, Gilmore's Band playing *Auld Lang Syne*, as it never has been played before in this city. So said those who have resided here since the metropolis was commenced.[13]

GILMORE'S SALEM BRASS BAND appears to have well sustained its reputation abroad. The Washington correspondent of the Boston Journal, writing on Tuesday, says:

"This morning, Gilmore's Band astonished the natives on Pennsylvania Avenue, as the Charlestown City Guard marched to the White House.— There they "stacked arms" and marched into the East Room, where Captain Pierce made a neat address to the President, who replied in his usual happy style. He then shook hands with every member of the corps, and introduced Gen. Shields, who was present. After re-forming out-of-doors, the Guard fired a salute, Gilmore's Band playing "Auld Lang Syne," as it never has been played before in this city. So said those who have resided here since the metropolis was commenced."

The Baltimore Sun says "their music is grand and inspiring—the time excellent."

The correspondent of the Post says:

Among the military visitors here the Charlestown City Guard, Capt. W. W. Pierce, are the most noticeable and the most admired. They number sixty-seven, as soldierly a set of men as can be found, I believe, throughout the Union.— Gilmore's Salem Brass Band, which accompanies them, attracts equal attention. Last evening the band serenaded Col. Charles G. Greene, and afterwards visited Georgetown, where they were invited in to something good by Major Ben. Perley Poore. Yesterday they also paid a visit to President Pierce.

The company reached Philadelphia, on their return, on Thursday afternoon, and received military courtesies both there and in Baltimore. They left Philadelphia on Saturday morning, remained in New York over Sunday, and will reach home tomorrow, via Lowell, where they will be received by the Watson Light Guards. In Charlestown extensive preparations have been made to welcome them.

Salem Register, March 9, 1857

Gilmore's contribution to President Buchanan's inauguration did not go unnoticed by Salem's local historian, Jim McAllister. He wrote on the SalemWeb blog:

The band's reputation earned it a highly sought-after invitation from the *New England Militia Company* to play at the inauguration of U.S. President James Buchanan. *The Salem Brass Band's* performance in the nation's capitol was praised by the Washington press, further enhancing its reputation as one of the nation's leading outfits. But the publicity also enraged the Boston area bands who had not been chosen to make the trip. Their egos were bruised, and a group of Bostonians decided to ambush Gilmore's group at the Boston train depot when they returned from Washington. The Bostonians planned to destroy the instruments of the Salem musicians and render their lips unserviceable for playing. Fortunately for the unsuspecting Salem band members, they caught an earlier train home and missed their surprise rendezvous with their jealous counterparts.[14]

Music Fills My Soul with Sadness/ Music is My Only Charm

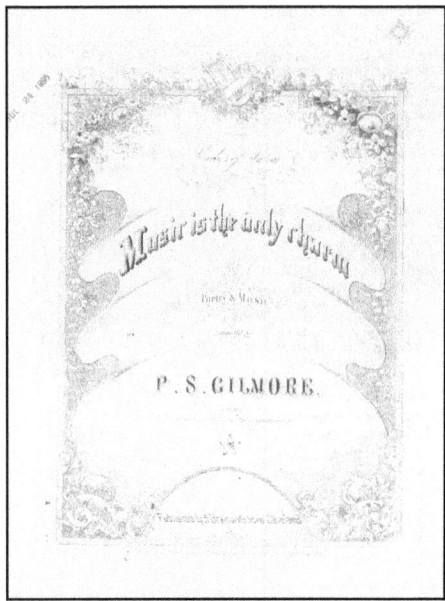

Music is My Only Charm,
courtesy of the University of Michigan

While leading the *Salem Brass Band*, Gilmore met his future wife, Miss Ellen J. O'Neill, while attending a concert led by the St. Patrick's Church Choir. O'Neill was living in Lowell, Massachusetts, and singing in St. Patrick's Church Choir. At first, Miss O'Neill had little interest in the older Gilmore. Gilmore responded to his sadness by writing the song *Music Fills My Soul With Sadness.* The *Salem Register* published the song on May 21, 1855. Gilmore officially published the song in 1856 and renamed it *Music is My Only Charm,* adding a chorus.[15]

Music is My Only Charm/
Music Fills My Soul with Sadness

Music Fills My Soul With Sadness
 Still, I fondly love its strain;
Once it brought me joy and gladness,
 Now, it seems to bring me pain.
'Tis because that link is broken,
 Friends no more in chorus join;
Music is the only Token,
 Of the joys that once were mine.

Chorus: Music fills my heart with sorrow,
 I fondly love its strain;
It may bring me joy tomorrow,
 Thou today it brings me pain.

Friends that I have loved and parted,
    Doomed on earth to meet no more;
Thoughts that leave me brokenhearted,
    Thoughts of joy that were before,
Once to me how dear and welcome,
    Sounds of merry songs and glee;
Give me now some sacred anthem,
    Southe my soul with harmony.

Chorus: Music fills my heart with sorrow,
    I fondly love its strain;
    It may bring me joy tomorrow,
    Thou today it brings me pain.

Hope still in my bosom lingers,
    Yet it brings no cheerful glow;
Blessed are the tuneful fingers,
    That can heal my heart from woe;
Music is the only charm,
    Let thy fingers gently sway;
Let me think my heart shall warm,
    To its joy some future day.

Chorus: Music fills my heart with sorrow,
    I fondly love its strain;
    It may bring me joy tomorrow,
    Thou today it brings me pain.

PATRICK S. GILMORE – 1855

For a brief period, Gilmore lived in Lowell, played cornet with the choir, and sang in St. Patrick's choir alongside Miss O'Neill. Gilmore wrote another song lamenting the fact they may never be together. The *Salem Register* included this little-known ballad in 1856 called *I Never Can Be Thine*.[16] There is minimal evidence on whether Gilmore officially published this song along with a corresponding tune. As time passed, their relationship grew, and the couple was married by Reverend John O'Brien, pastor of St. Patrick's Church. on May 13, 1858, in Lowell.

I Never Can Be Thine

Oh. no I never can be thine;
    Then bid the hopes depart,
And let thy thoughts to one incline,
    More worthy of thine heart.
I would not have thee shed a tear,
    Nor breathe a sign in vain;
Then go, and charm some other ear,
    Ne'er think of me again.

Go seek for one of higher birth
    Than fortune have to me;
Go choose a better home on earth
    Then I could hive to thee,
I will not tell thee, what I would
    If kingdoms were mine own;
But, blessed angel, if I could,
    I'd place thee on a throne.

The rich so seldom love the poor,
    How strange the act would be,
If one like thee could e'er endure
    To give thine hand to me.
Oh, no, 'twere better ne'er to wed
    Then choose the lot that's mine,
'Till I am numbered with the dead,
    I never can be thine.

Look up, there is a place above,
    Away from earthly woe;
A home of everlasting love,
    Where all the good shall go.
Then, let thy thoughts that would be mine,
    To Him on high he given,
On earth, I never can be thine,
    But, oh, I may in heaven.

PATRICK S. GILMORE – 1856

Gilmore's stay in Salem would end in 1858, but not without continued touring and publishing several additional song sheets, including *Everlasting Polka*,[17] *Norwich Cadet Polka*,[18] *Dinner Bell Polka*,[19] and the *Breakfast Bell Polka*.[20] Gilmore moved back to Boston to lead the *Boston Brigade Band*.

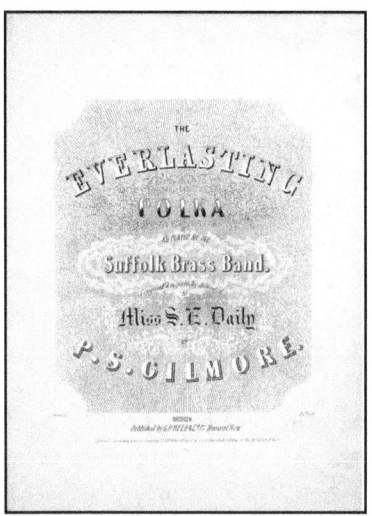

Everlasting Polka, courtesy of Lester S. Levy Collection of Sheet Music

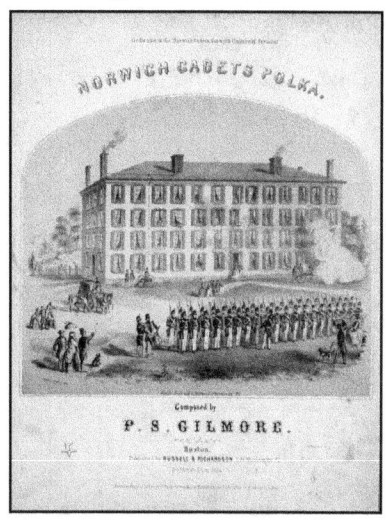

Norwich Cadet Polka, courtesy of Lester S. Levy Collection of Sheet Music

Breakfast Bell Polka, courtesy of Digital Commonwealth

Dinner Bell Polka, courtesy of Digital Commonwealth

On January 31, 1859, the *Salem Register* reported that Mr. J.H. Parsons, known for his excellent bugle and cornet playing, would take the leadership of the *Salem Brass Band* relinquished by P.S. Gilmore. [21]

When Johnny Comes Marching Home
Roud # 6673

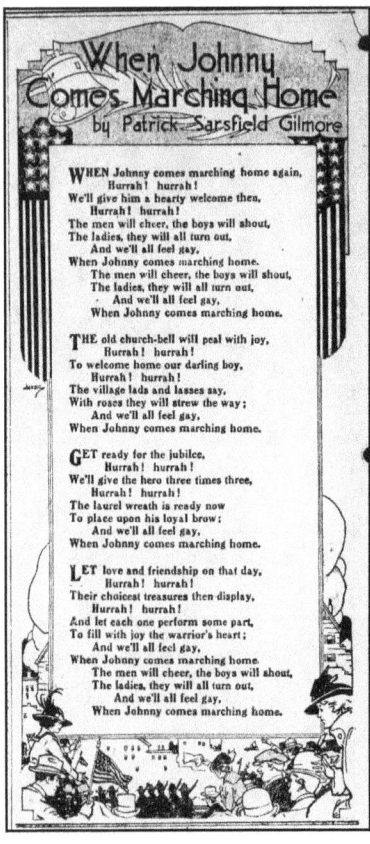

When Johnny Comes Marching Home,
Broadside, courtesy of Jarlath MacNamara

Patrick S. Gilmore wrote *When Johnny Comes Marching Home* under the pseudonym of Louis Lambert to celebrate a soldier returning home from the Civil War five years after leaving Salem. Gilmore did not write this song while he was in Salem, but its popularity and importance to the soldiers and their families on both sides of the war warranted inclusion. "It was inspired by the Battle of Gettysburg in July 1863 when the tide of the American Civil War began to turn in favor of the Union." [22] According to Margaret Bradford Boni, who wrote and compiled the *Fireside Book of Folk Songs*, Gilmore could have heard this tune when it was sung by an "African American," but as Boni pointed out, since Gilmore was an Irishman, it is more likely that the tune had Irish roots.[23] Louis Elson, writer of *The National Music of America and its Sources*, states that *Johnny Comes Marching Home* has a similar melody to the Irish songs *John Anderson, My Jo*, [24] and *Johnny, I Hardly Knew Ye*, an Irish protest song, As stated on the Library of Congress website, "It is possible that this air was written before Gilmore's *When Johnny Comes Marching Home* and that Gilmore unconsciously borrowed from the tune from an African-American spiritual." [25]

Discussion continues about the origins of this song.

When Johnny comes marching home again,
  Hurrah! Hurrah!
We'll give him a hearty welcome then,
  Hurrah! Hurrah!
The men will cheer and the boys will shout,
  The ladies they will all turn out,

And we'll all feel gay,
    When Johnny comes marching home.
And we'll all feel gay,
    When Johnny comes marching home.

The old church bell will peal with joy,
    Hurrah! Hurrah!
To welcome home our darling boy,
    Hurrah! Hurrah!
The village lads and lassies say,
    With roses, they will strew the way,
And we'll all feel gay,
    When Johnny comes marching home.
And we'll all feel gay,
    When Johnny comes marching home.

Get ready for the Jubilee,
    Hurrah! Hurrah!
We'll give the hero three times three,
    Hurrah! Hurrah!
The laurel wreath is ready now,
    To place upon his loyal brow,
And we'll all feel gay
    When Johnny comes marching home.
And we'll all feel gay,
    When Johnny comes marching home.

Let love and friendship on that day,
    Hurrah, hurrah!
Their choicest pleasures then display,
    Hurrah, hurrah!
And let each one perform some part,
    To fill with joy the warrior's heart,
And we'll all feel gay,
    When Johnny comes marching home.
And we'll all feel gay,
    When Johnny comes marching home.

LOUIS LAMBERT, AKA PATRICK S. GILMORE – 1863

Gilmore's World's Peace Jubilee

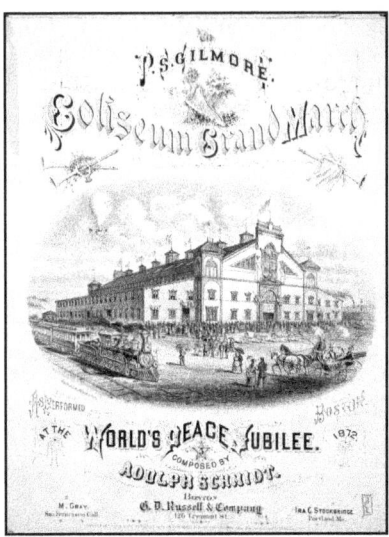

Coliseum Grand March, courtesy of the Boston Public Library

The *World's Peace Jubilee* took place in Boston, with the opening ceremonies on June 17, 1872, *Bunker Hill Day*, and ending on the 4th of July.[26] lasting over two weeks and consisted of a 2000-piece orchestra and a 20,000-voice chorus. It was the second of a series of performances commemorating the end of the Civil War and an effort to unite the country. The *National Peace Jubilee* took place on the weekend of June 15 – 19, 1869, before the *World's Peace Jubilee*. Gilmore directed both festivals.

Gilmore held the events in the *Boston Coliseum*. Constructed in the Back Bay of Boston and designed by William Preston, the *Boston Coliseum* was 550 in length and 350 feet wide and reached a height of 120 feet. Built as a temporary structure, the Coliseum was large enough to hold 100,00 people. The newly formed Jordan Marsh Company partially funded the building. [27]

Two groups that performed at the *World's Peace Jubilee* and received national and local attention were *The Fisk Jubilee Singers*, a group of black college students from *Fisk University* in Nashville, and according to the *Boston Daily Journal,* 100 Boston firemen were part of *Gilmore's Anvil Choir*. Under the direction of Gilmore, they performed *Verdi's Il Trovatore* and became local celebrities. [28]

Austrian-born Johann Strauss also performed at the Jubilee and conducted his composition *Beautiful Blue Danube*. The newspaper reported that the "selection was most beautifully rendered and was repeated at the enthusiastic demands of the Audience." [28]

Gilmore did not forget his days in Salem. At some point, he met music teacher and church organist Henry K. Oliver of Salem. Oliver is well known throughout Massachusetts. On a Tuesday evening, at the *World's Peace Jubilee,* with President Grant in attendance, Gilmore invited Oliver to "wield the baton" and lead the large orchestra and the chorus of 20,000, singing Oliver's newly composed hymn, *Hail, Gentle Peace*, written to the tune he called *Federal Street.* [29]

Henry K. Oliver

Henry K. Oliver, 1859,
courtesy of the Lawrence Public Library

Henry K. Oliver was born in Beverly, Massachusetts, on November 24, 1800, and died in Salem on August 12, 1885. Oliver served as the 21ˢᵗ Mayor of Salem from 1876 to 1880, the 5ᵗʰ mayor of Lawrence, Massachusetts, a member of the Massachusetts House of Representatives, an Adjutant General of Massachusetts, and the 26ᵗʰ Treasurer of Massachusetts. Oliver lived at 142 Federal Street, was a master of the theory and history of music, and was the author of several familiar compositions. The tune *Federal Street* has become permanent in musical literature and sacred harp singing.[30]

Federal Street
by Henry K. Oliver

Transcribed from the *Plain Dealer*, August 6, 1885
    How Oliver wrote *Federal Street*:
    "He was 31 years old when he sat in his library one afternoon reading Theodore Hook's novel, *Passion and Principle*." A passage suggested to him Mrs. Steele's lines, "So fades the lovely, blooming flower." As he ran through the last verse, "Thus gentle patience smiles on pain," an unbidden melody floated into his mind. He was not attempting composition, but without effort, words somehow melted into music. He sat quickly down at the piano and played the tune by improvising the harmonies. Then he transcribed it upon paper and threw it into a drawer. There, it lay for two years until Dr. Lowell Mason came to Salem to teach a class in music. Happening one day to ask if anyone present had ever written music, General Oliver thought of his composition and brought it forth. Dr. Mason asked for the privilege of publishing it in the academy collection. It was granted, but they were at a loss for a name. General Oliver promptly suggested, "Sally" that of his wife. But that would not do for a sacred tune, so *Federal Street*, the street on which the Olivers lived, was chosen, and the world has ever since been grateful to Henry K. Oliver for this grand old tune.[31]

Hail, Gentle Peace [32]

tune: *Federal Street*

Hail, gentle Peace! Good Will to Man!
    God's blessing o'er the world's wide span!
War's fearful storms are passed away,
    The Prince of Peace o'er earth bears sway.

No sounds of battle rend the air,–
    No shrieks of passion or despair;
But, from the woods, the vales, the hills,
    Sweet Peace the air with music fills.

So the full choir of angels bright,
    Heralds of Christ, ere early light,
To shepherds sang melodious strains,
    On the still air of Bethlehem's plains.

Take up, ye voices, all the song,
    With high acclaim the strain prolong;
Earth, join to angel choir your voice,
    And in full harmony rejoice.

HENRY K. OLIVER – 1872

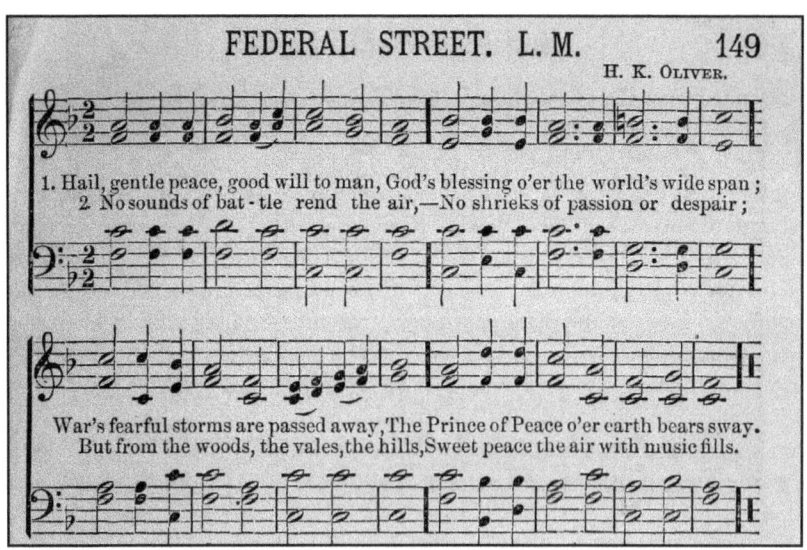

*Hail Gentle Peace, The Devotional Chimes: A Collection of New
& Standard Hymns, courtesy of the Boston Public Library* [33]

18

– Obituary –

Death of the well-known band leader
and organizer of the World's Peace Jubilee.

Patrick S. Gilmore

Transcribed from *The Boston Journal*, September 26, 1892:[34]

Patrick Sarfield Gilmore, the famous band leader and organizer of the World's Peace Jubilee, died in St. Louis on Saturday of heart disease due to indigestion.

Mr. Gilmore had been feeling unwell for several days and consulted a local doctor, who treated him for indigestion. On Saturday afternoon, for the first time since the beginning of his present engagement at the exposition in St. Louis, he did not occupy his usual place and wield the baton at the band's concert.

Mr. Gilmore's remains were taken to New York on Sunday, accompanied by his wife and daughter, Miss Minnie, the only immediate members of his family who were present at the time of his death.

Patrick S. Gilmore was born on Christmas Day 1829 in County Galway, Ireland. At the age of fifteen, Gilmore became a music teacher in Ireland. At nineteen, he packed up his musical instruments and sailed for Boston. He soon became known as a cornet player and was invited to play in the Charlestown band.

Soon afterward, he became leader of the *Suffolk Band* of Boston, succeeding Edward Kendall, the bugler. John Bartlett, the trumpeter and leader of the *Brigade Band*, died, and Mr. Gilmore was asterned in his place. Then Jerome Smith of the *Salem Band* died, and there was another opening, to which Mr. Gilmore succeeded.

By this time, he had made a name as the E Flat cornet player of the entire country. He was a member of the *Salem Band* for three years and, while serving in that capacity, conceived the idea of fathering the Boston Common Fourth of July Concert and the promenade concerts given at the Music Hall. Gilmore returned to Boston in 1858, where his projects were worked out.

When the war broke out, he and his band went to the front with the *Twenty-fourth Massachusetts Volunteers*. Service in the cause found Gilmore in New Orleans in 1864, where all the bands and music in military deployment were placed under his charge. There it was that he organized what may be styled as his first, great Jubilee, the occasion being the restoration of civic power under the Stars and Stripes in that city. He projected the pain of having a chorus of 10,000 school children and 500 musicians, with infantry and artillery accompaniment, in a grand national concert to aid in the inauguration of Michael Hahn, the first Governor of Louisiana elected under the Union administration just before the close of the war. A few years later, he conceived the idea of the *National Peace Jubilee* held in Boston.

OBITUARY.

P. S. GILMORE.

Death of the Well-Known Band Leader and Originator of the World's Peace Jubilee.

Patrick Sarsfield Gilmore, the famous band leader and originator of the World's Peace Jubilee, died in St. Louis Saturday of heart disease due to indigestion.

Mr. Gilmore had been several days feeling unwell and consulted a local doctor, by whom he was treated for indigestion. Saturday afternoon, for the first time since the beginning of his present engagement at the exposition in St. Louis, he did not occupy his usual place and wield the baton at the band's concert.

Mr. Gilmore's remains were taken to New York Sunday. They were accompanied by his wife and daughter, Miss Minnie, the only immediate members of his family who were present at the time of his death.

Patrick S. Gilmore was born on Christmas Day, 1830, in the County Galway, Ireland. At the age of fifteen Gilmore became a music teacher in Ireland. At the age of nineteen he packed up his musical instruments and sailed for Boston. He soon became known as a cornet player, and was invited to play in the Charlestown Band.

Soon afterward he became leader of the Suffolk Band of Boston, succeeding Edward Kendall, the bugler.

John Bartlett, the trumpeter and leader of the Brigade Band, died, and to Mr. Gilmore was assigned his place. Then Jerome Smith of the Salem Band died, and there was another opening, to which Mr. Gilmore succeeded.

He had by this time made a name as the E flat cornet player of the country. He was a member of the Salem Band for three years, and while serving in that capacity conceived the idea of fathering the Boston Common Fourth of July concerts, also the promenade concerts, afterward given at Music Hall. In 1858 he returned to Boston where his projects were worked out.

When the war broke out he and his band went to the front with the Twenty fourth Massachusetts Volunteers. Service in the cause found Gilmore at New Orleans in 1864, where all the bands and music in the military department were placed under his charge. Here it was that he organized what may be styled his first great Jubilee, the occasion being the restoration of civil power under the Stars and Stripes in that city. He projected the plan of having a chorus of 10,000 school children and 500 musicians, with infantry and artillery accompaniments, in a grand national concert to use the inauguration of Michael Hahn, the first Governor of Louisiana elected under the Union administration just before the close of the war. A few years later he conceived the idea of the great "National Peace Jubilee," which was held in Boston.

Three years after the first Jubilee, which was entirely national in character, Gilmore yearned for a musical gathering which should represent all nations. With this idea, he visited the chief Governments of Europe, the result being that in 1872, Boston was again the centre of attraction for the eyes and ears of all musical Christendom. Never in the world's history had there been such a gathering of musicians? The chorus numbered 20,000 voices, and the great orchestra numbered 2000 instrumentalists. In addition to these, the Band of the Grenadier Guards from London came to represent the British, the Band of the Garde Republicaine from Paris, the French, and the Band of the Kaiser Franz Regiment from Berlin, the Germans, while Johann Straus stood up for the "Blue Danube" and Austria.

The accomplishment of these great Jubilees gave Gilmore a universal fame. New York became now the Mecca of Gilmore's ambition, and in 1874 he moved to that city and organized the Twenty second Regiment Band.

In 1880 and 1887 he filled a protracted engagements with the great exposition in St. Louis. During the last engagement, on the occasion of the triennial conclave of Knights Templar of the country at St. Louis in September of this year, he organized a mammoth band, consisting of organizations brought to St. Louis by the knights, numbering 2000 musicians, and gave a concert attended by 120,000 people.

Mr. Gilmore possessed the valuable quality of geniality of temperament as well as musical talent.

Three years after the first Jubilee, which was entirely national, Gilmore yearned for another musical gathering that should represent all nations. With this idea, he visited the chief Governments of Europe, the result being that in 1872, Boston was again the center of attraction for the eyes and ears of all musical Christendom. Never in the world's history had been such a gathering of musicians? The chorus numbered 20,000 voices, and the orchestra numbered 2,000 instrumentalists. In addition, the Band of Grenadier Guards from London came to represent the British, the Band of the Garde Republic came from Paris, the French and the Band of the Kaiser Franz Regiment from Berlin, the Germans, while Johann Straus stood up for the "Blue Danube" and Austria.

The accomplishment of these great Jubilees gave Gilmore universal fame. New York became now the Mecca of Gilmore's ambition, and in 1874, he moved to that city and organized the *Twenty-second Regiment Band*.

In 1880 and 1887, he filled a protracted engagement with the great exposition in St. Louis. During the last engagement, on the occasion of the triennial conclave of Knights Templar of the country at St. Louis in September of this year, he organized a mammoth band consisting of organizations brought to St. Louis by the Knights, numbering 2,000 musicians and gave a concert attended by 120,000 people.

Mr. Gilmore possessed the valuable quality of geniality of temperament, as well as musical talent.

Patrick S. Gilmore's Obituary,
The Boston Journal,
September 26, 1892

A PARTIAL LIST OF PATRICK S. GILMORE'S PUBLISHED COMPOSITIONS

1853 *On the Road to Salem Quick Step: Salem Hornpipe*
1854 *Exquisite Polka*
Good News From Home
Sad News From Home
1855 *Come Buy the Bridal Ring*
Oh, Let Me Dream of Former Years
The Prize Baby Polka
1856 *Bonnie Woman's Smile*
Music Fills My Soul With Sadness
Music is the Only Charm
1857 *The New England Guards Polka*
Norwich Cadets Polka
The Bewitching Polka
Grape Vine Polka
1858 *The Breakfast Bell Polka*
The Dinner Bell Polka
The Supper Bell Polka
Sons of Temperance Quick Step
1859 *Astor House Polka*
Academy Polka
Empire Polka
1860 *When Johnny Comes Marching Home*
1861 *God Save the Union: National Anthem*
The Voice of a Departing Soul
1862 *We are Coming Father Abraam*
1863 *The Spirit of the North: Patriotic Song*
1866 *Emblem Schottische*
Freedom on the Old Plantation
1868 *How Beautiful the Light of Home:*
   words Dexter Smith;* music P.S. Gilmore
1869 *Let Us Have Peace*

[*Dexter Smith, composer with strong family ties to Salem, Massachusetts – RS]

ENDNOTES

Patrick S. Gilmore: Time in Salem 1855 – 1858

1. Marwood Darlington, *Irish Orpheus, The Life of Patrick S. Gilmore Bandmaster Extraordinary* (Philadelphia: Oliver, Maney, Klien Co. 1950), 35.
2. Patrick S. Gilmore, *Sad News From Home*: a ballad/poetry and music. (Boston: Geo. P. Reed & Co., 1854).
3. *Salem Register*, January 15, 1855.

The Early Days of the *Salem Brass Band*

4. "The Early Days of The Salem Brass Band," *Salem Register*, March 3, 1859.

Salem Hornpipe (On the Road to Salem)

5. Patrick Sky, ed., *Ryan's Mammoth Collection Fiddle Tunes* (Pacific, MO: MelBay Publication, 1995, originally published in Boston, 1883), 120 & *On The Road To Salem*, Patrick Gilmore (Boston: G.P. Reed & Co., 1853).
6. Jim Dalton, "Gilmore's Road To Salem," *Salem Gazette*, June 3, 2010.

Gilmore Concerts with the *Salem Brass Band*

7. *Boston Herald*, March 30, 1855
8. "Grand Concert," *Salem Register*, July 28, 1856.
9. *The Salem Brass Band*, Concert poster, Smith Family Scrapbook.
10. "Program at Gallows, Hill," *Salem Register*, July 28, 1856.
11. Grand Concert Broadside, Gilmore's *Salem Brass Band,* 1856.
12. *Salem Register,* March 2, 1857
13. *Salem Register,* March 9, 1857
14. Jim McAllister, *Patrick Gilmore, and the Salem Brass Band*, Salem Web, Retrieved on-line January 1, 2024, https://salemweb.com/about-salem/salem-tales/patrick-gilmore/

Music is My Only Charm/Music Fills My Soul with Sadness

15. *Salem Register*, May 21, 1855, & Gilmore, P. S. (Patrick Sarsfield), 1829-1892. *Music Is the Only Charm* (Cleveland: S. Brainard's Sons, 1856).

I Never Can Be Thine

16. "I Never Can Be Thine," *Salem Register,* March 3, 1856.
17. Patrick Sarsfield Gilmore, *The Everlasting Polka* (Boston: G.P. Reed & Co., 17 Tremont Row, 1852).

18. Patrick S. Gilmore, *Norwich Cadet Polka* (Cleveland: S. Brainard's Sons, 1856).
19. Patrick Sarsfield Gilmore, *Dinner Bell Polka* (Boston: Russell & Tolman, 291 Washington St., 1855).
20. Patrick S. Gilmore, *Breakfast Bell Polka* (Chicago, IL: Will A. Pratt, 1856).
21. *Salem Register*, January 31, 1859.

When Johnny Comes Marching Home
22. Marwood Darlington, *Irish Orpheus: The Life of Patrick S. Gilmore, Bandmaster Extraordinary* (Philadelphia: Oliver, Maney, Klein, Co. 1950), 35.
23. Margaret Bradford Boni, *Fireside Book of Folk Songs* (New York: Simon and Schuster, 1947), 198.
24. Louis Charles Elson, *The National Music of America and its Sources* (Boston: L.C. Page and Company, 1900), 248.
25. Louis Lambert, *When Johnny Comes Marching Home Again*. Library of Congress, Washington, DC, 2002. retrieved online September 31, 2017. Library of Congress, https://www.loc.gov/item/ihas.200000024/.

World's Peace Jubilee
26. *Boston Daily Advertiser,* Thursday, August 10, 1871.
27. Patrick Sarsfield Gilmore: *History of the National Peace Jubilee and Great Musical Festival: Held in the City of Boston, 1869.* Illustrated with Steel Engravings (New York: Lee, Shepard, and Dillingham, 1871).
28. *Boston Daily Journal,* Saturday, June 08, 1872 Boston, MA.
29. Henry K. Oliver, *Hail, Gentle Peace, Salem Register*, July 1, 1872.

Henry K. Oliver
30. Dauan Hamilton Hurd, *History of Essex County, Massachusetts: With Biographical Sketches of Many of Its Pioneers and Prominent Men, Volume 1, part 1* (Philadelphia, PA: J. W. Lewis & Co. 1888), 227.
31. *Plain Dealer*, August 6, 1885.

Hail, Gentle Peace
32. Henry K. Oliver, *Hail, Gentle Peace, Salem Register*, July 1, 1872.

Federal Street
33. Henry K. Oliver, *Federal Street* – tune, *Hail Gentle Peace, The Devotional Chimes: A Collection of New & Standard Hymns* (Philadelphia, Asa Hull, 1873), 149.

Obituary, Patrick S. Gilmore,
34. *Boston Journal*, September 26, 1892.

INDEX

BIBLIOGRAPHY

Boni, Margaret Bradford. *Fireside Book of Folk Songs.* New York: Simon and Schuster, 1947.

Cole's Thousand Fiddle Tunes. Chicago, IL: M. M. Cole Publishing Co., 1967.

Cipolla, Frank. *Patrick S. Gilmore: The Boston Years and Beyond.* Kongressbericht Abony Ungarn: Herausgegeben von Wolfgang Suppan. Tutzing: Verlegt Bei Hans Schneider, 1996.

Darlington, Marwood. *Irish Orpheus: The Life Of Patrick S. Gilmore, Bandmaster Extraordinary.* Philadelphia: Oliver, Maney, Klein, Co., 1950.

Elson, Louis Charles. *The National Music of America and its Sources* Boston: L.C. Page and Company, 1900.

Emilio, Luis F. *A Brave Black Regiment 1863-1865.* Boston: Boston Book Company, 1894.

Ewen, David, ed. *American Popular Songs from the Revolutionary War to the Present.* New York: Random House, 1966.

Gilmore, P. S., and J.H. Bufford's Lith. *Breakfast Bell Polka.* Cleveland: S. Brainard's Sons, 1868.

Gilmore, Patrick Sarsfield. *Dinner Bell Polka,* Boston: Russell & Tolman, 291 Washington St., 1855. Lester Levy Sheet Music Collection, John Hopkins University

Gilmore, Patrick Sarsfield. *The Everlasting Polka.* Boston: G.P. Reed & Co., 17 Tremont Row, 1852. Lester Levy Sheet Music Collection, John Hopkins University

Gilmore, Patrick Sarsfield. *Essex Institute Historical Collection*, XXXVI. Salem Mass.: Printed for the Essex Institute, 1900.

Gilmore, P. S. *Hail Gentle Peace. The Devotional Chimes: A Collection of New & Standard Hymns.* Philadelphia: Hull Asa, 1873.

Gilmore, P. S. *Music Is the Only Charm.* Cleveland: S. Brainard's Sons, 1856.

Gilmore, P. S. *On the Road to Salem Quick Step.* Boston: Geo. P Reed, Tremont Road, Boston, 1853.

Gilmore, P. S. *Sons of Temperance Quick Step.* Boston: Russell & Fuller, 1858.

Gilmore, P. S. *The History of Peace Jubilee.* Boston: Lee and Shepard, 1871.

Gilmore, Patrick Sarsfield. *Sad News From Home: a Ballad.* Boston: Geo. P. Reed & Co., 1854.

Goldman, Richard. *The Wind Band: Its Literature and Technique.* Boston: Allyn and Bacon, reprint 1961.

Lambert, Louis. *When Johnny Comes Marching Home Again.* Boston: Henry Tolman & Co., 1863.

MacNamara, Jarlath. *With Perfect Pitch-Patrick Sarsfield Gilmore.* NYIHR V27-02, Vol. 27, 2013. https://nyirishhistory.us/article/with-perfect-pitch-patrick-sarsfield-gilmore/

Owen, Ann. editor. Ouren, Todd, illustrator. *Gilmore, Patrick S. When Johnny Comes Marching Home.* Minneapolis, Minnesota: Picture Window Books, 2003.

Schmidt, Adolph. *Coliseum Grand March.* Boston: G.D. Russell & Co, 1872.

Sky, Patrick. editor. *Ryan's Mammoth Collection Fiddle Tunes.* Pacific. MO: MelBay Publication, 1995.

WEB RESOURCES:

Boston College, John J. Burns Library, Michael Cummings Collection of P.S. Gilmore Materials.
https://libguides.bc.edu/burns

Broadside: *When Johnny Comes Marching Home,* Ephemera Collection of Jarlath MacNamara
https://thewildgeese.irish/profiles/blog/list?user=3oefbthtmnd4u

Digital Commonwealth
https://www.digitalcommonwealth.org/

New York Irish History: *With Perfect Pitch: Patrick S. Gilmore*
https://nyirishhistory.us/article/with-perfect-pitch-patrick-sarsfield-gilmore/

Salem Public Library, Salem Links and Lore, Salem History Room, Salem, MA
https://salempl.org/

HathiTrust
https://www.hathitrust.org/

PHOTOGRAPHS, POSTCARDS, CLIPPINGS, MAPS

Patrick S. Gilmore, *Irish World,* August 23, 1890
Patrick S. Gilmore, *Essex Institute Historical Collectio*n, Salem Public Library
Sad News From Home, Patrick S. Gilmore, Lester S. Levy Collection of Sheet
   Music, Sheridan Libraries, Johns Hopkins University
On the Road to Salem, Patrick S. Gilmore, & Phillips
   Library, Rowley, MA
Salem Hornpipe, Ryan's Mammoth Collection, Jim and Maggi Dalton's
   personal collection
Music and Dancing, *Boston Herald*, March 30, 1855
Grand Concert, *Salem Register,* July 28, 1856
The Salem Brass Band, Concert poster, Smith (Burnham) Family Scrapbook
Program at Gallows Hill, *Salem Register,* July 28, 1856
Grand Concert – Gilmore's *Salem Brass Band*, Jarlath MacNamara
   personal collection
Off to Washington, *Salem Register*, March 2, 1857
Gilmore's Salem Brass Band, *Salem Register*, March 9, 1857
Music is My Only Charm, Patrick S. Gilmore, University of Michigan
The Everlasting Polka, Patrick S. Gilmore, Lester S. Levy Collection of Sheet
   Music, Sheridan Libraries, Johns Hopkins University
Norwich Cadet Polka, Patrick S. Gilmore, Lester S. Levy Collection of Sheet
   Music, Sheridan Libraries, Johns Hopkins University
Dinner Bell Polka, Patrick S. Gilmore, Digital Commonwealth
Breakfast Bell Polka, Patrick S. Gilmore, Digital Commonwealth
When Johnny Comes Marching Home, Patrick S. Gilmore, Jarlath MacNamara
Coliseum Grand March, Patrick S. Gilmore, Boston Public Library
Henry K. Oliver, Lawrence Public Library
*Hail Gentle Peace, The Devotional Chimes: A Collection of New & Standard
   Hymns,* Boston Public Library
Obituary, P.S. Gilmore, *The Boston Journal*, September 26, 1892

ACKNOWLEDGMENT

I want to express my gratitude to my wife, Jennifer, for her support throughout this process for her work at the Salem Public Library and for developing the Wiki link, Salem Links and Lore, a local source for Salem history found on the Salem Public Library's website. I am thankful to Cynthia Napierkowski, Salem resident and long-time Salem High School Band Leader and Salem Community Band Director. Thank you to Jim McAllister for sharing his vast knowledge of Salem's history with the Salem community. Appreciations to Professor of Music Theory at the Boston Conservatory, Jim Dalton, and Jarlath MacNamara for his deep interest in the life of Patrick S. Gilmore and for allowing access to his vast collection of Gilmore material.

I would like to thank the following libraries for their knowledge, support, and the use of their material: Boston Public Library, Digital Public Library of America, John J. Burns Library at Boston College, Lester S. Levy Collection of Sheet Music at John Hopkins University, Phillips Library Rowley, Massachusetts, Salem Public Library, University of Maryland Libraries, University of Michigan and the HathiTrust.

Lastly, I would like to acknowledge all my music friends, local pub sessions, and our local community singing groups and bands who support and keep live music in their lives and for sharing a love of music and community.

Keep on singing!
Bob

Salem Community Band Leader
Cynthia Napierkowski's (biographical profile)

Cynthia Napierkowski has been teaching in the Salem Public Schools since 1987, filling numerous music educator roles for 35 years. She holds a Bachelor's Degree in Music from UMass Amherst and an M. Ed. degree from Cambridge College. Cynthia has received various awards for music education, including the *George N. Parks Leadership in Music Education Award* and the *J. Michael Ruane Community Service Award.*

APPENDIX

The appendix was added to help students gain a further understanding of the songs and tunes that Gilmore wrote and published while he was in Salem.

Academy Polka
> Gilmore, P. S. (Patrick Sarsfield), 1829-1892. *Academy Polka*: As Per formed by Gilmore's Band. Boston: Gilmore & Russell, 1859.

The Bewitching Polka
> Gilmore, P. S. (Patrick Sarsfield), 1829-1892. *The Bewitching Polka*. Cleveland: S. Brainard's Sons, 1857.

Good News From Home
> Gilmore, P. S. (Patrick Sarsfield), 1829-1892. *Good News From Home*: Ballad, As Sung by *Ordway's Aeolians*, Geo. *Christy & Woods Minstrels, West & Peel's Campbell Minstrels, Christy's Minstrels* and Other Celebrated Vocalists Throughout the Union. Boston: Henry Tolman & Co., 1854.

Grape Vine Polka
> Gilmore, P. S. (Patrick Sarsfield), 1829-1892. *Grape Vine Polka*: for the Piano. Cleveland: S. Brainard's Sons, 1857.

Music is the Only Charm
> Gilmore, P. S. (Patrick Sarsfield), 1829-1892. *Music Is the Only Charm*. Cleveland: S. Brainard's Sons, 1856.

New England Guard Polka
> Gilmore, P. S. (Patrick Sarsfield), 1829-1892. *The New England Guards Polka*. Cleveland: S. Brainard's Sons, 1857.

Oh Let Me Dream of Former Years
> Gilmore, P. S. (Patrick Sarsfield), 1829-1892. *Oh Let Me Dream of Former Years*: Song & Chorus. Cleveland: S. Brainard's Sons, 1855.

Sad News From Home
> Gilmore, P. S. (Patrick Sarsfield), 1829-1892. *Sad News From Home*: a Ballad. Boston: Geo. P. Reed & Co., 1854.

ACADEMY POLKA.

To the

Ladies of Salem.

THE

Bewitching

POLKA

by

P. S. Gilmore.

Published by S. Brainard's Sons, Cleveland.

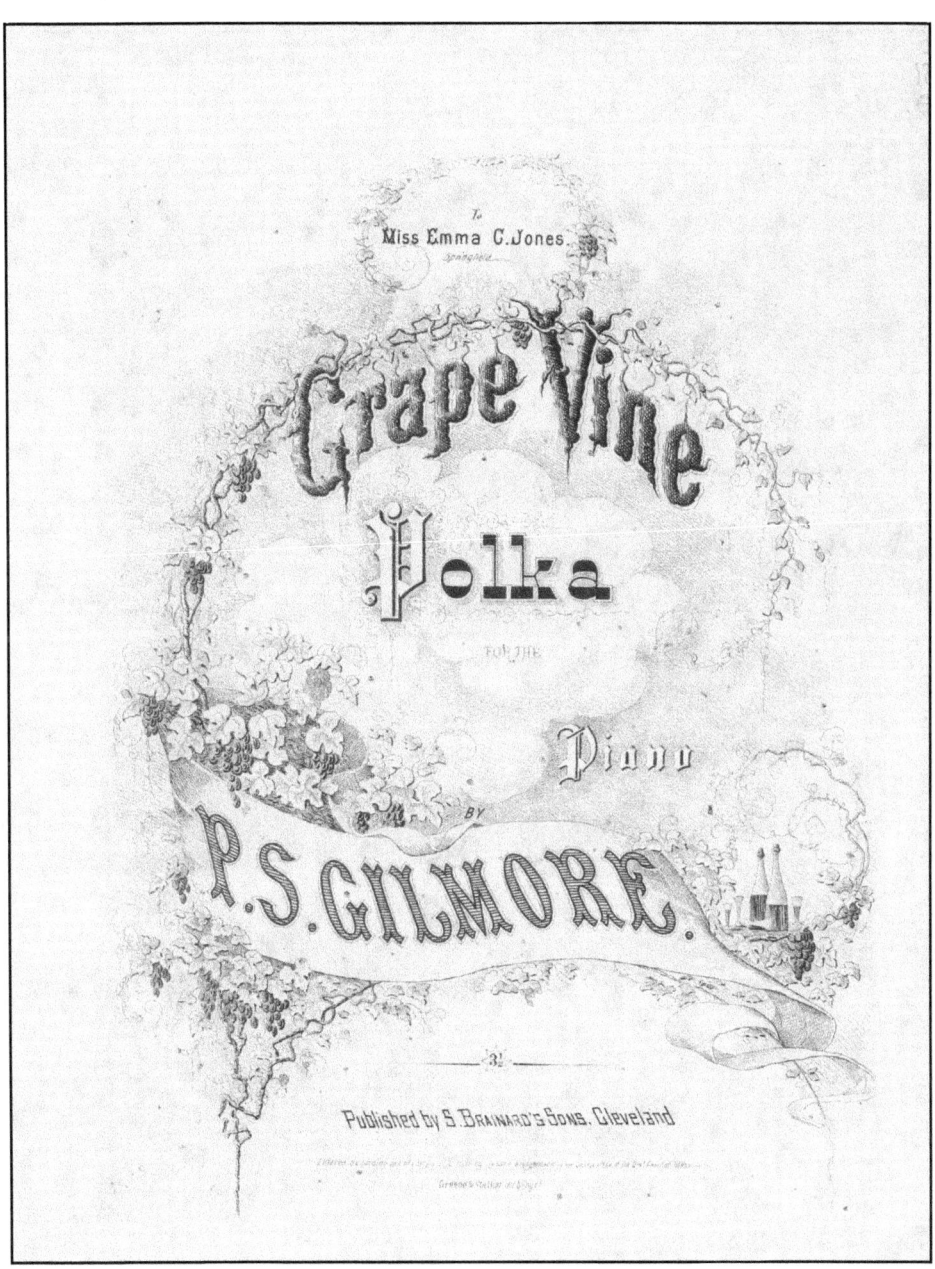

49

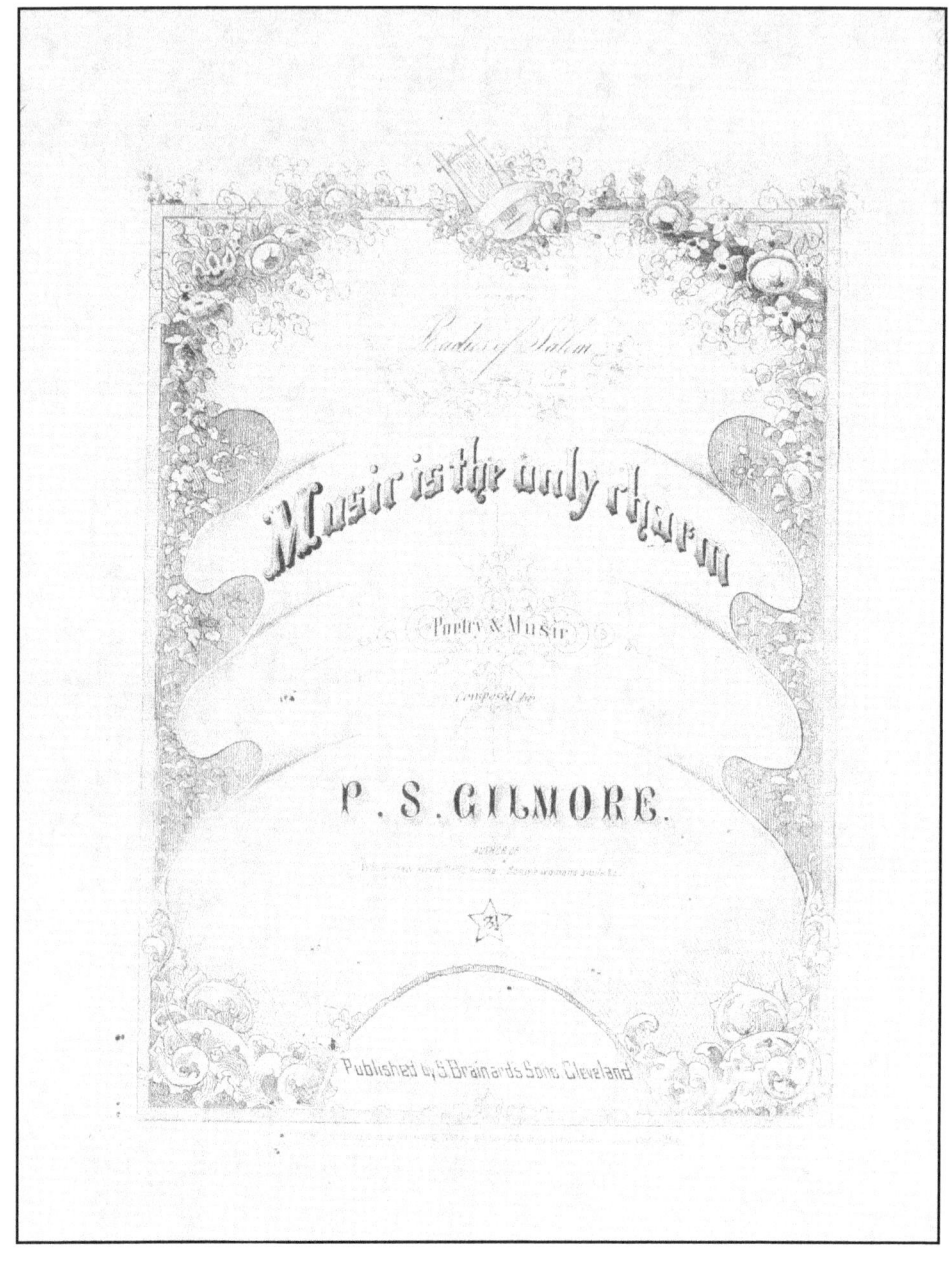

To Capt. Geo T. Lyman.

THE

New England Guards

POLKA

By

P. S. Gilmore.

Published by S. Brainard's Sons Cleveland.

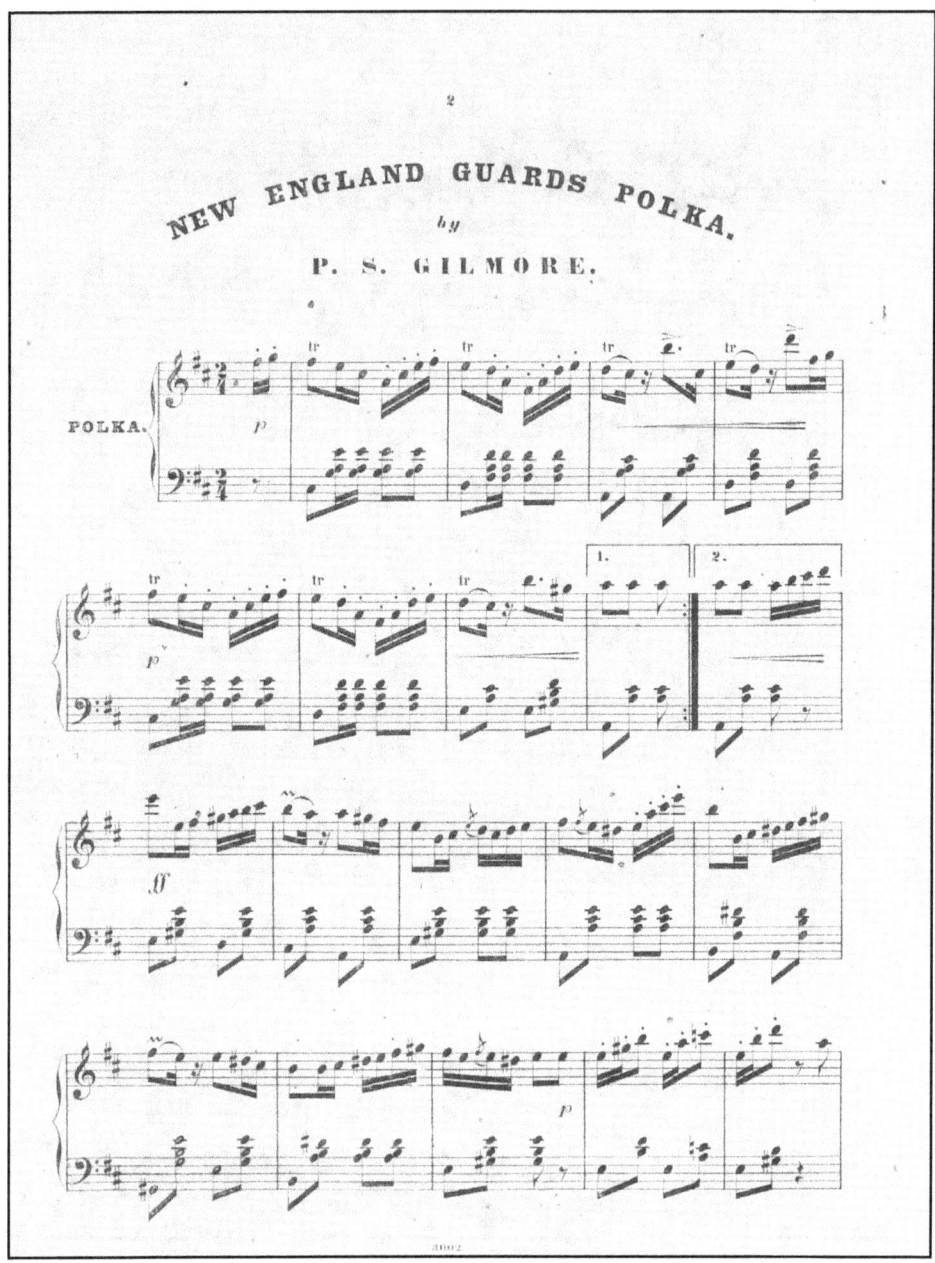

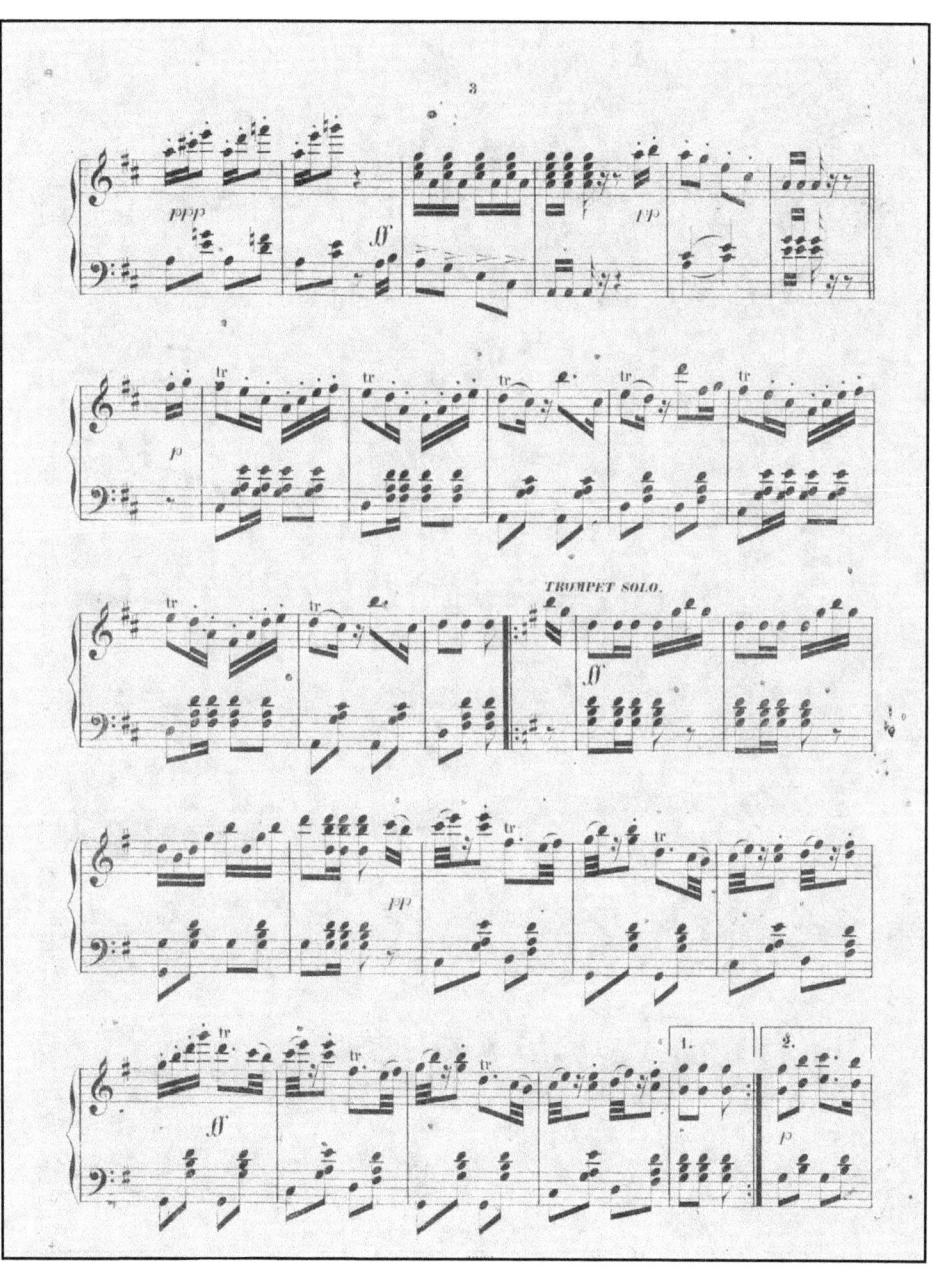

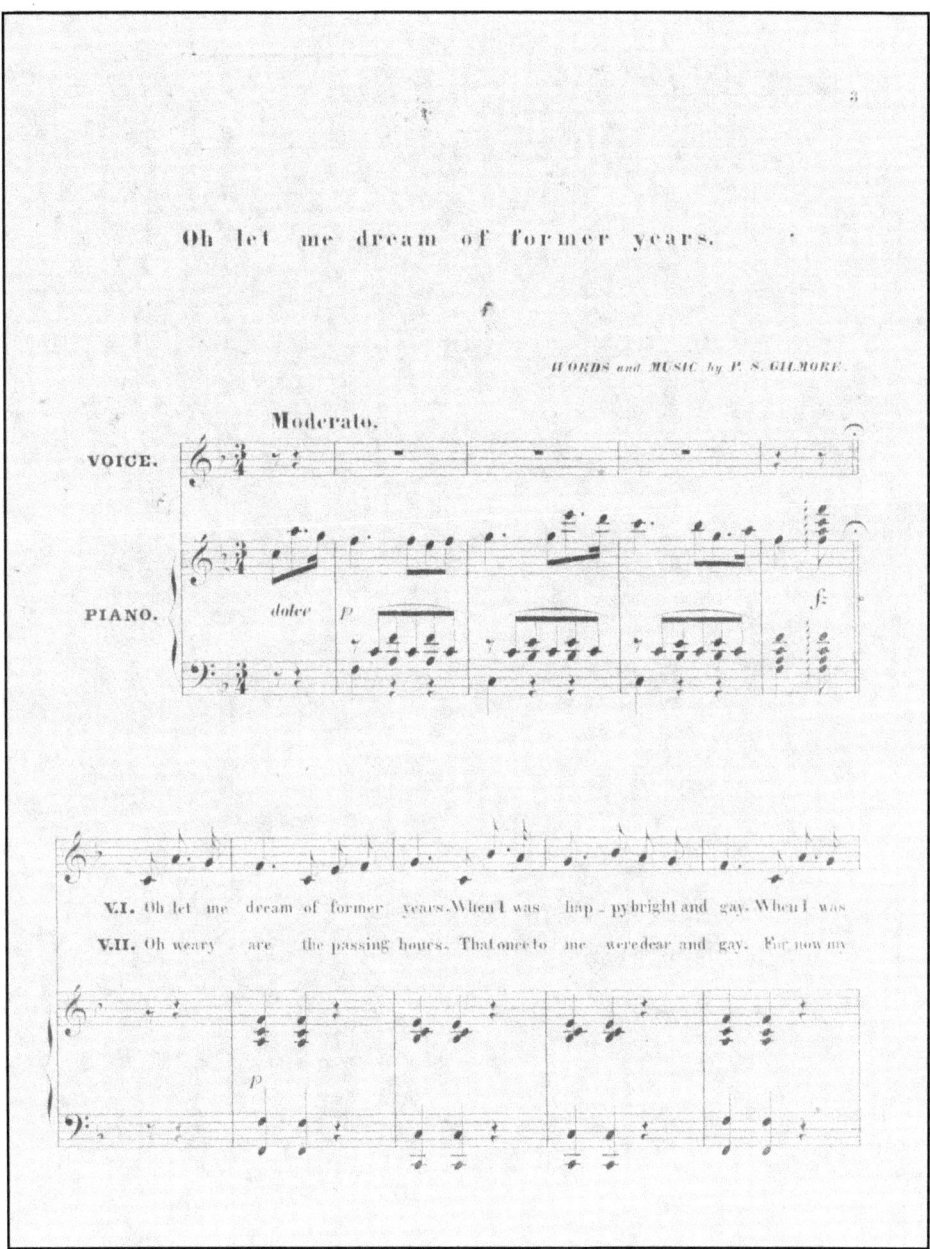

Oh let me dream of former years.

WORDS and MUSIC by P. S. GILMORE.

V.I. Oh let me dream of former years. When I was happy, bright and gay. When I was

V.II. Oh weary are the passing hours. That once to me were dear and gay. For now my

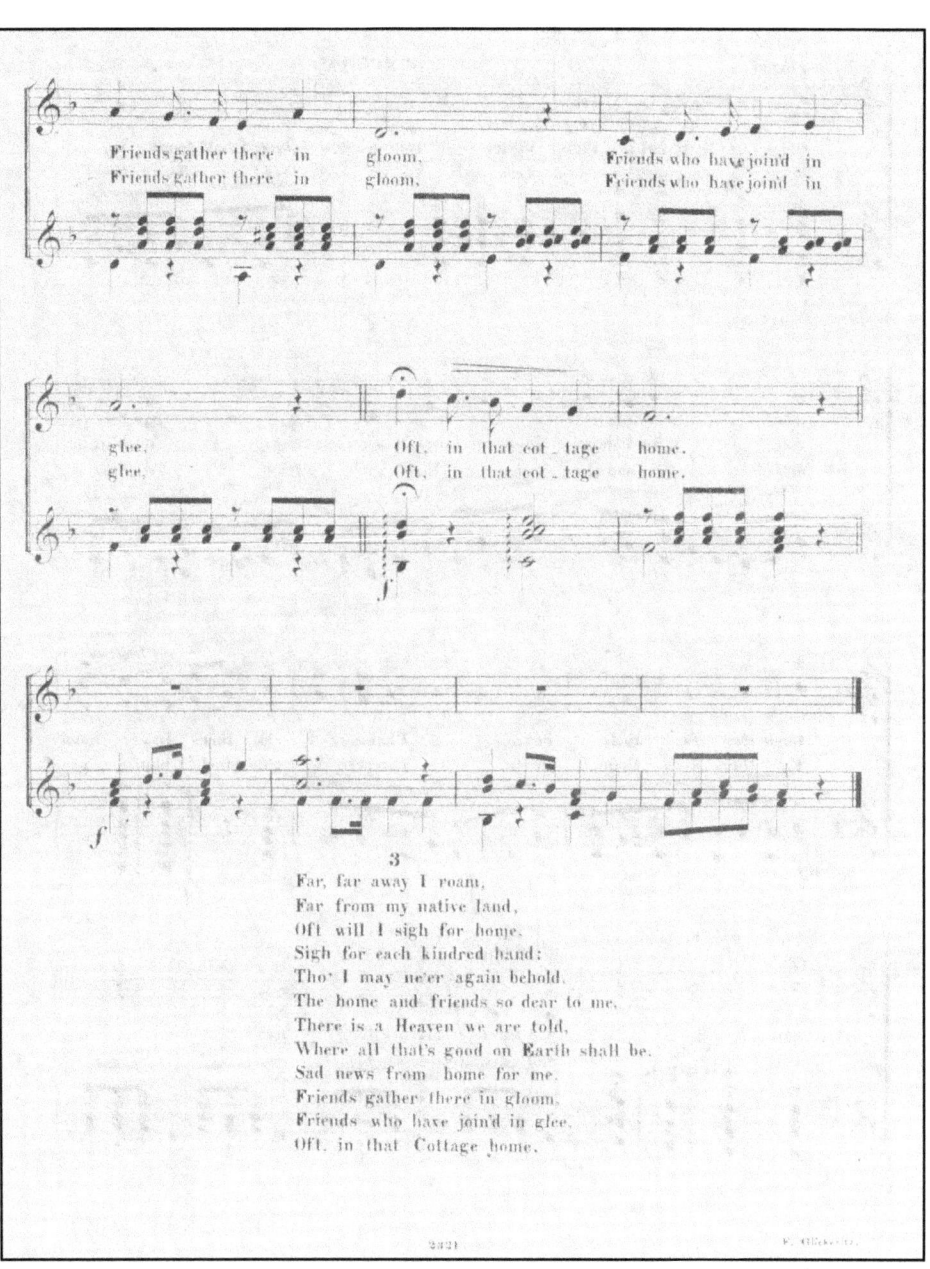

3
Far, far away I roam,
Far from my native land,
Oft will I sigh for home,
Sigh for each kindred band;
Tho' I may ne'er again behold,
The home and friends so dear to me,
There is a Heaven we are told,
Where all that's good on Earth shall be.
Sad news from home for me,
Friends gather there in gloom,
Friends who have join'd in glee.
Oft, in that Cottage home.

www.ingramcontent.com/pod-product-compliance
Lightning Source LLC
Chambersburg PA
CBHW071344130626
46556CB00005B/2014